AF504446

Jamaican Proverbs for Children + Activities

By Dr. Cornelia Walters-Jones

No part of this publication may be reproduced, stored in retrieval system, or transmitted in any mean, e.g. electronic, photocopy, recording- without the prior written permission of the author. The only exception is brief quotation in printed reviews/and presentations.

Printing or ordering information
Dr. Cornelia Walters-Jones
Tel: 876-836-0000
Email: labrish@jamaicangyal.com
website: drcorneliawaltersjones.com

ISBN: 9798324503031

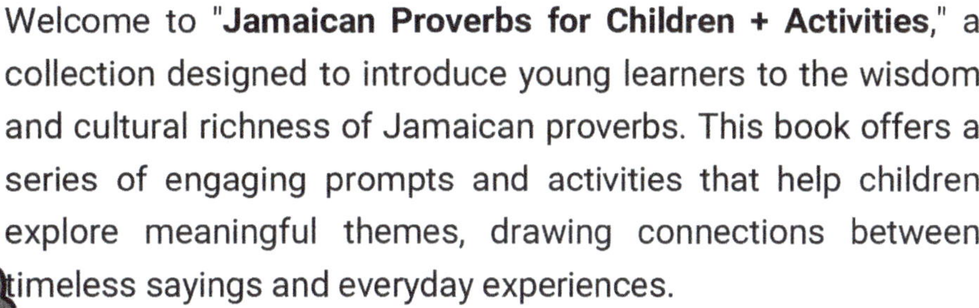

Welcome to "**Jamaican Proverbs for Children + Activities**," a collection designed to introduce young learners to the wisdom and cultural richness of Jamaican proverbs. This book offers a series of engaging prompts and activities that help children explore meaningful themes, drawing connections between timeless sayings and everyday experiences.

Each activity in this collection is crafted to deepen understanding of Jamaican culture while fostering critical thinking and emotional growth. From writing stories that illustrate the importance of patience and perseverance to drawing scenes that capture the essence of human kindness and resilience, this book is a treasure trove of lessons that are both educational and culturally enriching.

In "**Jamaican Proverbs for Children + Activities**," you will find activities such as:

"**The Depths Within**": A story-writing prompt that uses the proverb "It is only when you are closely involved with some persons that you are able to really know them" to teach the importance of empathy and deeper understanding.

"**Baxter's Bone Bonanza**": An illustration and reflection activity based on the idea of moderation, inspired by the saying "Take just what you can comfortably manage, rather than attempt to grab everything for yourself."

Lessons from the Art Project": A narrative exercise that helps children learn to accept their mistakes and move forward, drawing from the wisdom of "What's done is done."

"**Grandpa's Garden Wisdom**": A drawing and story-writing activity that connects young readers with the wisdom of older generations, fostering respect and appreciation for lifelong learning through the eyes of Jamaican proverbs.
Each chapter begins with a setup that includes the proverb, guiding questions, and a proposed activity that integrates drawing or writing. The book also offers moral reflections to help children and educators discuss and digest the lessons learned from each activity.

"**Jamaican Proverbs for Children + Activities**" is more than just a book; it's a journey into the heart of Jamaican heritage. It's about understanding that each challenge and every mistake is a stepping stone to becoming more thoughtful, resilient, and empathetic individuals. Whether used in the classroom or at home, these activities provide valuable cultural insights in creative and accessible ways, ensuring that the journey of learning is as enjoyable as it is educational.

Embark on this culturally enriching journey with us, where each page turns into an opportunity to learn more about the complexities of life and the unique joys of Jamaican culture.

3

Tideh
fi yuh,
tommorow fi mi,
what dat mean?

WHAT DAT MEAN?

TIDEH FI MI TOMORROW FI YUH.
EVERYONE WILL FACE PROBLEMS OR ACHIEVE SUCCESS IN HIS OR HER OWN TIME.

ACTIVITY: PLANTING PATIENCE

INSTRUCTION:

IMAGINE WE PLANT TWO SEEDS: ONE GROWS VERY QUICKLY, AND THE OTHER TAKES A LONG TIME TO SPROUT.

CAN YOU DRAW WHAT YOU THINK EACH PLANT WILL LOOK LIKE IN A WEEK? WHAT ABOUT IN A MONTH? WHY DO YOU THINK THEY GROW DIFFERENTLY?"

What dawg knam yuh suppa mean?

WHAT DAT MEAN?

DAWG KNAM YUH SUPPA:
IF YOU ARE NOT CAREFUL WITH WHAT YOU HAVE,
YOU WILL LOSE IT.

Writing time

ACTIVITY: THE ADVENTURE OF THE MISSING TOY

INSTRUCTIONS:
IMAGINE YOUR FAVORITE TOY HAS GONE ON AN
UNEXPECTED ADVENTURE BECAUSE YOU DIDN'T
PUT IT AWAY PROPERLY. NOW IT'S MISSING

WRITE A STORY ABOUT WHAT HAPPENS TO THE
TOY WHILE IT'S MISSING. WHERE DID IT GO? WHO
DID IT MEET? WHAT ADVENTURES DID IT HAVE?!

Who caan dance seh di music nuh good, what dat mean?

WHAT DAT MEAN?

WHO CAAN DANCE SEH DI MUSIC NUH GOOD:

WHEN A PERSON IS UNABLE TO DO OR DONT KNOW HOW TO DO SOMETHING, THEY   PLACE THE BLAME OR FIND EXCUSES.

Writing time

ACTIVITY: THE HOMEWORK MYSTERY

INSTRUCTIONS:

IMAGINE A CLASSMATE, ALEX, WHO DIDNT DO THEIR HOMEWORK BECAUSE THEY FOUND IT TOO DIFFICULT. INSTEAD OF ASKING FOR HELP, ALEX DECIDES TO COME UP WITH VARIOUS EXCUSES.

WRITE A STORY WHERE THEY ARE A DETECTIVE FIGURING OUT WHY ALEX DIDNT DO THEIR HOMEWORK. THROUGHOUT THE STORY, THEY UNCOVER DIFFERENT EXCUSES ALEX MAKES.

Tief nuh
love fi tief wid
long bag, what
dat mean?

WHAT DAT MEAN?

TIEF NUH LOVE FI SI TIEF WID LONG BAG:

THOSE WHO PROSPER BY ILLEGAL OR CROOKED MEANS DISLIKE THOSE WHO ARE MORE SUCCESSFUL THAN THEMSELVES VIA THE SAME MEANS.

Speaking time

ACTIVITY: THE CHEATING CHAMPIONSHIP

INSTRUCTIONS:

IMAGINE A SCHOOL SPORTS DAY WHERE TWO STUDENTS, JAMIE AND CASEY, DECIDE TO CHEAT IN A RACE TO WIN. BOTH OF THEM USE SHORTCUTS TO TRY TO FINISH FIRST.

1. HOW DO JAMIE AND CASEY FEEL WHEN THEY SEE THE OTHER CHEATING?

2. WHAT DO THE OTHER STUDENTS THINK WHEN THEY FIND OUT ABOUT THE CHEATING?

A NUH
every mango
hab maggic, what
dat mean?

WHAT DAT MEAN?

A NUH EVERY MANGO HAB MAGGIC:
IN LIFE, NOT ALL SITUATIONS WILL STAY BAD OR DIFFICULT. GOOD WILL COME TO YOU, SO DONT GIVE UP, KEEP ON GOING.

ACTIVITY: TURNAROUND TALES

INSTRUCTIONS:

THINK OF A TIME WHEN SOMETHING STARTED OUT DIFFICULT OR UNHAPPY FOR THEM, BUT THEN IT GOT BETTER BECAUSE THEY KEPT TRYING AND DIDNT GIVE UP.

PREPARE A SHORT STORY TO READ TO THE CLASS. WHAT WAS THE PROBLEM OR DIFFICULT SITUATION YOU FACED?

- WHAT ACTIONS DID YOU TAKE TO TRY TO MAKE THINGS BETTER?
- HOW DID THE SITUATION CHANGE AFTER YOU KEPT TRYING?
- WHAT DID YOU LEARN FROM THIS EXPERIENCE?

When water throw weh it cant pick up, what dat mean?

WHAT DAT MEAN?

WHEN WATER THROW WEH IT CANT PICK UP:
WHAT'S DONE IS DONE.

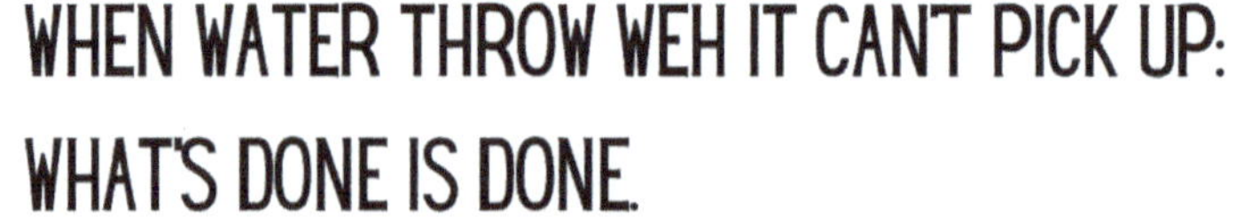

<u>ACTIVITY:</u> LESSONS FROM THE ART PROJECT

<u>INSTRUCTIONS:</u>

IMAGINE A CHARACTER NAMED CASEY WHO IS WORKING ON A MAJOR ART PROJECT FOR SCHOOL. IN A RUSH TO FINISH, CASEY MAKES A SIGNIFICANT MISTAKE THAT CANNOT BE UNDONE AND MUST PRESENT THE PROJECT AS IS.

WRITE A STORY ABOUT CASEY DEALING WITH THE CONSEQUENCES OF THE ART PROJECT MISTAKE. EXPLORE HOW CASEY HANDLES THE INITIAL DISAPPOINTMENT AND THE REACTIONS FROM TEACHERS AND CLASSMATES.

When yuh guh a fireside an see food eat half and left half. What dat mean?

WHAT DAT MEAN?

WHEN YUH GO A FIRESIDE AN SEE FOOD, EAT HALF AN LEF HALF: DONT FINISH ALL YOU HAVE ONE TIME, PREPARE FOR THE DAYS YOU WONT HAVE.

ACTIVITY: THE GREAT SNACK SAVE

INSTRUCTIONS:

IMAGINE YOU HAVE A BIG BOX OF YOUR FAVORITE SNACKS, ENOUGH TO LAST A WHOLE WEEK. BUT, THERE'S A TWIST! YOU CANT GO TO THE STORE TO GET MORE UNTIL NEXT WEEK.

WRITE A STORY ABOUT HOW YOU PLAN TO USE YOUR SNACKS FOR THE WHOLE WEEK. DESCRIBE EACH DAY, FROM MONDAY TO SUNDAY, AND TELL US WHAT YOU DECIDE TO EAT EACH DAY. THINK ABOUT HOW YOU MAKE SURE YOU STILL HAVE SNACKS BY THE END OF THE WEEK.

Hot neegle bun thread, what dat mean?

WHAT DAT MEAN?

HOT NEEGLE BUN THREAD:
IMPATIENCE CAN RUIN THE OUTCOME OF WHAT YOU WANT.

<u>ACTIVITY:</u> THE RUSHED ART PROJECT

<u>INSTRUCTIONS:</u>

IMAGINE YOU'RE IN ART CLASS AT SCHOOL, AND TODAY'S PROJECT IS TO CREATE THE MOST BEAUTIFUL PAINTING YOU CAN. THE TEACHER HAS TOLD EVERYONE THAT THERE'S PLENTY OF TIME AND THAT TAKING YOUR TIME WILL MAKE YOUR PAINTING EVEN BETTER.

WRITE A STORY ABOUT A STUDENT NAMED SAM WHO IS VERY EXCITED AND WANTS TO FINISH FIRST. SAM STARTS RUSHING THROUGH THE PAINTING, WANTING TO BE THE FASTEST RATHER THAN THE BEST. DESCRIBE WHAT HAPPENS TO SAM'S PAINTING BECAUSE OF THE HURRY.

Book learning a nuh intelligence, what dat mean?

WHAT DAT MEAN?

BOOK LEARNING A NUH INTELLIGENCE:

BECAUSE SOMEONE IS WELL-EDUCATED DOESNT MEAN THEY HAVE COMMON SENSE.

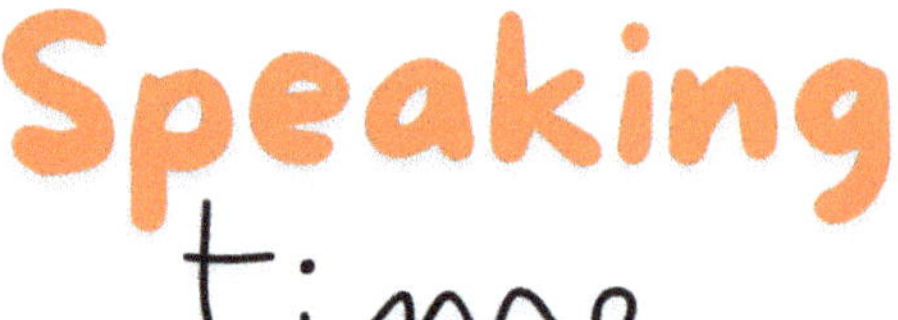

<u>ACTIVITY:</u> THE GENIUS WHO COULDNT COOK

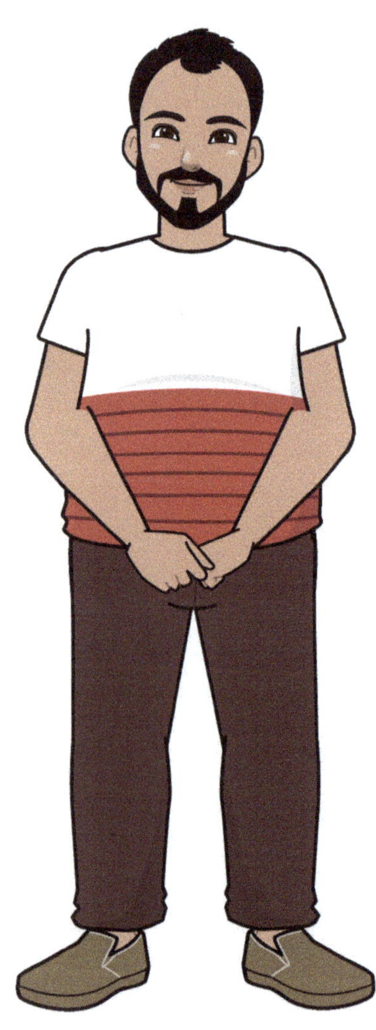

<u>INSTRUCTIONS:</u>

IMAGINE THERE'S A VERY SMART TEACHER NAMED MR. SMARTYPANTS, WHO KNOWS A LOT ABOUT BOOKS, STARS, AND NUMBERS. HE'S KNOWN FOR BEING THE MOST EDUCATED PERSON IN TOWN. ONE DAY, HE DECIDES TO COOK A SIMPLE MEAL FOR HIS FRIENDS.

TELL A STORY ABOUT MR. SMARTYPANTS'S COOKING ADVENTURE. DESPITE HIS VAST KNOWLEDGE, HE STRUGGLES WITH BASIC COOKING TASKS LIKE BOILING WATER, MEASURING INGREDIENTS, OR SETTING THE RIGHT TEMPERATURE ON THE OVEN. DESCRIBE THE FUNNY MISHAPS THAT HAPPEN ALONG THE WAY.

Howdy and tenku nuh broke nuh square, what dat mean?

WHAT DAT MEAN?

HOWDY AND TENKU NUH BRUK NUH SQUARE:

IT DOES NO HARM TO SHOW GOOD MANNERS TO PEOPLE.

Speaking time

ACTIVITY: THE MAGIC WORDS ADVENTURE

INSTRUCTIONS:

IMAGINE THAT THERE'S A MAGICAL WORLD WHERE THE POWER OF GOOD MANNERS CAN MAKE INCREDIBLE THINGS HAPPEN. THIS WORLD IS VISITED BY A KIND BUT FORGETFUL BOY NAMED TOBY, WHO SOMETIMES FORGETS TO USE HIS MANNERS.

TELL A STORY ABOUT TOBY'S DAY IN THE MAGICAL WORLD. THROUGHOUT HIS ADVENTURE, DESCRIBE HOW DIFFERENT SITUATIONS TURN OUT DEPENDING ON WHETHER HE REMEMBERS TO SAY "PLEASE," "THANK YOU," "EXCUSE ME," OR "I'M SORRY." SHOW SPECIFIC INSTANCES WHERE TOBY'S USE OF MANNERS HELPS HIM MAKE NEW FRIENDS, FIND HIDDEN PATHS, OR EVEN UNLOCK MAGICAL POWERS.

Little
axe cut down
big tree, what
dat mean?

WHAT DAT MEAN?

LITTLE AXE CUT DOWN BIG TREE:
THE MIGHTY CAN BE TAKEN DOWN BY SOMEONE SMALL.

ACTIVITY: DAVID AND THE MIGHTY GIANT

INSTRUCTIONS:

IMAGINE A PEACEFUL VILLAGE PROTECTED BY A GENTLE GIANT NAMED GOLIATH. ONE DAY, GOLIATH STARTS CAUSING TROUBLE INSTEAD OF HELPING. THE VILLAGERS ARE TOO SCARED TO CONFRONT HIM BECAUSE OF HIS SIZE AND STRENGTH.

WRITE A STORY ABOUT A YOUNG VILLAGER NAMED DAVID WHO IS NOT AS PHYSICALLY STRONG AS GOLIATH BUT IS CLEVER AND BRAVE. DAVID DECIDES TO STAND UP TO GOLIATH USING HIS WIT AND SOME SIMPLE TOOLS.

Nuh
tek ugly mek
laugh, what dat
mean?

WHAT DAT MEAN?

NUH TEK UGLY MEK LAUGH:
DONT LAUGH AT THE MISFORTUNE OF OTHERS.

Speaking time

ACTIVITY: THE DAY LAUGHTER TURNED LESSONS

INSTRUCTIONS:

IMAGINE A SCHOOL WHERE A NEW RULE IS INTRODUCED: IF SOMEONE LAUGHS AT ANOTHER PERSON'S MISFORTUNE, THEY MUST SPEND A DAY IN THE OTHER PERSON'S SHOES TO UNDERSTAND THEIR FEELINGS.

TELL A STORY ABOUT A STUDENT NAMED JAMIE WHO LAUGHS WHEN ANOTHER STUDENT, ALEX, TRIPS AND SPILLS THEIR LUNCH IN THE CAFETERIA. BECAUSE OF THE NEW RULE, JAMIE HAS TO SPEND A DAY EXPERIENCING LIFE AS ALEX, WHO FACES MANY SMALL CHALLENGES EVERY DAY.

Talk
and taste yuh
tongue, what
dat mean?

WHAT DAT MEAN?

TALK AND TASTE YUH TONGUE:
THINK BEFORE YOU SPEAK.

ACTIVITY: THINK BEFORE YOU
SPEAK

<u>FIND THESE WORDS</u>

ADVICE

LISTEN

SILENT

THINK

WISE

WORDS

L C B M P W E
K I L E H O C
F N S C E R I
J I I T V D V
W M O H E S D
L Y K I T N A
T N E L I S H

Hog seh di first duty water mi ketch mi wash, what dat mean?

WHAT DAT MEAN?

HOG SEH DI FIRST DUTY WATER MI KETCH, MI WASH:

MAKE USE OF THE FIRST OPPORTUNITIES THAT COMES YOUR WAY – INSTEAD OF WAITING FOR THE IDEAL ONE.

Writing time

ACTIVITY: THE RACE TO RAINBOW'S END

INSTRUCTIONS:

IMAGINE A STORY WHERE THERE'S A RACE TO FIND THE END OF A RAINBOW, RUMORED TO HAVE A TREASURE. MANY PARTICIPANTS WAIT FOR THE PERFECT SUNNY DAY TO START THEIR JOURNEY, THINKING IT WILL BE EASIER TO SEE THE RAINBOW.

WRITE A STORY ABOUT A CHARACTER NAMED CHARLIE WHO DECIDES TO START SEARCHING RIGHT AFTER A RAINSTORM, EVEN THOUGH CONDITIONS AREN'T PERFECT. OTHER CHARACTERS WAIT FOR WHAT THEY THINK WILL BE THE IDEAL DAY.

Likkle
but talawah,
what dat
mean?

WHAT DAT MEAN?

LIKKLE BUT TALAWAH:
SMALL BUT ABLE TO DO ANYTHING WE SET OUR MINDS TO.

ACTIVITY: TINY HEROES, BIG DREAMS

INSTRUCTIONS:

IMAGINE A TINY VILLAGE WHERE ALL THE CREATURES ARE NO BIGGER THAN A THUMB. DESPITE THEIR SIZE, THESE TINY VILLAGERS HAVE BIG DREAMS AND HUGE HEARTS.

WRITE A STORY ABOUT A YOUNG CHARACTER FROM THIS VILLAGE, NAMED PIP, WHO DREAMS OF ACHIEVING SOMETHING THAT SEEMS IMPOSSIBLE FOR SOMEONE SO SMALL LIKE CLIMBING THE TALLEST FLOWER IN THE GARDEN, WHICH TO THEM IS AS TALL AS A SKYSCRAPER.

33

What
nuh kill fatten,
what dat mean?

WHAT DAT MEAN?

WHAT NUH KILL FATTEN:

WHAT DOESNT KILL YOU, FATTENS YOU. WHEN YOU ENDURE DIFFICULTY WITHOUT DYING YOU ALWAYS EMERGE STRONGER THAN BEFORE.

Drawing time

ACTIVITY: THE GREAT GARDEN CHALLENGE

INSTRUCTIONS:

IMAGINE A YOUNG SQUIRREL NAMED SAMMY WHO LIVES IN A VAST AND BEAUTIFUL GARDEN. SAMMY FACES A TOUGH WINTER WHERE FOOD IS SCARCE AND SURVIVAL IS CHALLENGING.

DRAW A PICTURE OF ONE OF SAMMY'S CLEVER SOLUTIONS TO A PROBLEM OR A SCENE SHOWING HOW HE HAS CHANGED BY THE END OF WINTER.

Kin
teeth kibba
heart bun, what
dat mean?

WHAT DAT MEAN?

TEK KIN TEET KIBBA HEART BUN:

WHEN IN DIFFICULTIES, A LITTLE LAUGHTER CAN HELP YOU TO FEEL BETTER ABOUT YOUR PROBLEMS.

ACTIVITY: THE LAUGHTER CLUB

INSTRUCTIONS:

IMAGINE A SCHOOL WHERE THE STUDENTS DISCOVER THAT LAUGHING TOGETHER CAN HELP THEM FEEL BETTER WHEN THEY'RE FACING TOUGH TIMES, LIKE A BIG TEST OR A DIFFICULT DAY.
WRITE A STORY ABOUT A GROUP OF FRIENDS WHO DECIDE TO START A "LAUGHTER CLUB" AT THEIR SCHOOL. EVERY TIME ONE OF THEM IS HAVING A HARD DAY, THEY MEET DURING LUNCH TO TELL JOKES, MAKE FUNNY FACES, OR SHARE SILLY STORIES.

When
dog hab money
him buy cheese,
what dat mean?

WHAT DAT MEAN?

WHEN DOG HAVE MONEY HIM BUY CHEESE:

WHEN PEOPLE HAVE A LOT OF MONEY, THEY BUY THINGS THAT THEY DONT NEED.

ACTIVITY: THE SHOPPING SPREE ADVENTURE

INSTRUCTIONS:

IMAGINE A CHARACTER NAMED MAX WHO SUDDENLY FINDS A TREASURE CHEST FILLED WITH GOLD COINS IN HIS BACKYARD. EXCITED BY THIS NEWFOUND WEALTH, MAX DECIDES TO GO ON A MASSIVE SHOPPING SPREE.

DRAW A PICTURE OF MAX IN A STORE SURROUNDED BY ALL THE THINGS HE BOUGHT THAT HE DOESNT NEED.

Tom
drunk, Tom
nuh fool, what
dat mean?

WHAT DAT MEAN?

TOM DRUNK BUT TOM NO FOOL:
SOMEONE PRETENDING TO BE INNOCENT TO GAIN KNOWLEDGE.

Writing time

ACTIVITY: THE CLEVER NEWCOMER

INSTRUCTIONS:

IMAGINE A CHARACTER NAMED LILY WHO HAS JUST JOINED A NEW SCHOOL. LILY PRETENDS TO KNOW LESS THAN SHE ACTUALLY DOES ABOUT VARIOUS SUBJECTS, HOPING TO HEAR DIFFERENT EXPLANATIONS AND PERSPECTIVES FROM HER TEACHERS AND CLASSMATES.

WRITE A STORY ABOUT LILY'S EXPERIENCES AS SHE NAVIGATES HER CLASSES, INTERACTING WITH TEACHERS AND PEERS WHILE MAINTAINING HER FACADE OF INNOCENCE.

Wise monkey know which tree fi climb, what dat mean?

WHAT DAT MEAN?

WISE MONKEY KNOW WHICH TREE TO CLIMB:
SET ACHIEVABLE GOALS AND CREATE A PLAN TO OBTAIN THEM.

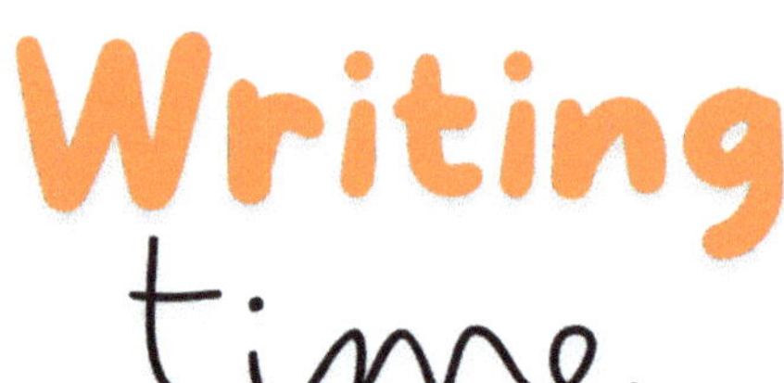

ACTIVITY: MIA'S BIG DREAM

INSTRUCTIONS:

IMAGINE A CHARACTER NAMED MIA WHO HAS A BIG DREAM TO BECOME A CHAMPION SWIMMER. HOWEVER, SHE'S JUST A BEGINNER AND NEEDS TO FIGURE OUT HOW TO ACHIEVE HER DREAM STEP BY STEP.

WRITE A STORY ABOUT MIA'S JOURNEY FROM BEING A BEGINNER TO ACHIEVING HER GOAL OF BECOMING A CHAMPION. DESCRIBE THE SPECIFIC GOALS SHE SETS FOR HERSELF AND THE DETAILED PLAN SHE CREATES TO REACH EACH OF THOSE GOALS.

Time
longer dan
rope, what dat
mean?

WHAT DAT MEAN?

TIME LONGER THAN ROPE:
THIS ENCOURAGES ONE TO BE PATIENT AND TO WORK HARD AND WAIT UNTIL YOU TIME COMES.

ACTIVITY: LEO'S LONG WAIT FOR THE PERFECT SHOT

INSTRUCTIONS:

IMAGINE A YOUNG ASPIRING PHOTOGRAPHER NAMED LEO WHO DREAMS OF TAKING THE PERFECT WILDLIFE PHOTOGRAPH TO WIN A YOUNG PHOTOGRAPHERS' COMPETITION. HOWEVER, THE PERFECT OPPORTUNITY TO CAPTURE SUCH A PHOTO COMES VERY RARELY.

WRITE A STORY ABOUT LEO'S YEAR-LONG JOURNEY, DETAILING HIS PATIENCE AND THE HARD WORK HE PUTS INTO IMPROVING HIS PHOTOGRAPHY SKILLS WHILE WAITING FOR THE PERFECT OPPORTUNITY TO TAKE HIS DREAM PHOTO.

A nuh
lack a tong mek
cow nuh talk, what
dat mean?

WHAT DAT MEAN?

A NUH LACK A TONGUE MEK COW NUH TALK:
IT'S ALWAYS BEST TO BE DISCREET; IT'S NEVER GOOD TO GOSSIP.

Writing time

<u>ACTIVITY:</u> THE SECRET KEEPER'S PROMISE"

<u>INSTRUCTIONS:</u>

IMAGINE A CHARACTER NAMED EMMA WHO IS KNOWN AMONG HER FRIENDS AS A TRUSTWORTHY SECRET KEEPER. ONE DAY, EMMA OVERHEARS A RUMOR ABOUT A NEW STUDENT IN CLASS AND FACES A DILEMMA ABOUT WHETHER TO SHARE IT OR KEEP IT TO HERSELF.

WRITE A STORY ABOUT EMMA'S INTERNAL CONFLICT AND THE DECISION SHE MAKES REGARDING THE GOSSIP. EXPLORE THE CONSEQUENCES OF HER ACTIONS, WHETHER SHE CHOOSES TO SHARE THE RUMOR OR KEEP IT TO HERSELF.

Scawnful dog knam dutty pudding, what dat mean?

WHAT DAT MEAN?

SCORNFUL DOG KNAM DUTTY PUDDING:

YOU COULD EASILY FIND YOURSELF IN THE SAME SITUATION YOU CRITICIZED IN THE PAST.

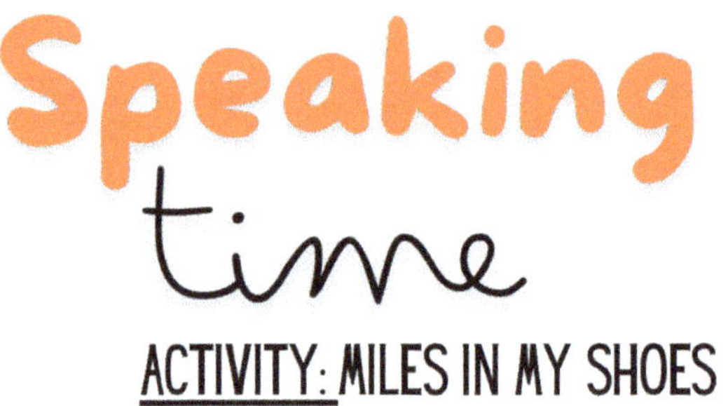

Speaking time

ACTIVITY: MILES IN MY SHOES

INSTRUCTIONS:

IMAGINE A CHARACTER NAMED JAMIE WHO IS KNOWN FOR BEING QUICK TO JUDGE OTHERS. JAMIE OFTEN CRITICIZES OTHER STUDENTS FOR THINGS LIKE NOT DOING WELL ON A TEST OR FORGETTING THEIR HOMEWORK. ONE DAY, JAMIE FINDS THEMSELVES IN A SIMILAR SITUATION THEY HAD PREVIOUSLY CRITICIZED.

TELA STORY ABOUT JAMIE'S EXPERIENCE WHEN THEY END UP FACING THE SAME CHALLENGES AS THOSE THEY JUDGED. DESCRIBE THE INITIAL JUDGMENT, THE TURN OF EVENTS THAT LEADS JAMIE TO A SIMILAR SITUATION, AND THE REACTION FROM OTHERS.

Yuh caan plant corn an expect fi reap peas, what dat mean?

WHAT DAT MEAN?

YUH CAAN PLANT CORN AND EXPECT FI REAP PEAS:
YOU REAP WHAT YOU SOW. WHAT EVER YOU PUT IN IS WHAT YOU
WILL RECEIVE.

Writing time

ACTIVITY: THE GARDEN OF EFFORT

INSTRUCTIONS:

IMAGINE A SCHOOL PROJECT WHERE EACH STUDENT IS GIVEN A PLOT IN THE SCHOOL GARDEN TO PLANT AND TAKE CARE OF FOR A WHOLE SEASON. EACH STUDENT CAN CHOOSE WHAT THEY WANT TO PLANT AND MUST MANAGE THEIR PLOT INDEPENDENTLY.

WRITE A STORY ABOUT A CHARACTER NAMED ALEX WHO, UNLIKE THEIR CLASSMATES, DECIDES TO PUT MINIMAL EFFORT INTO THEIR GARDEN PLOT. DESCRIBE THE INITIAL CHOICES ALEX MAKES, THE EFFORTS (OR LACK THEREOF) PUT INTO MAINTAINING THE PLOT, AND COMPARE THE OUTCOMES WITH THOSE OF CLASSMATES WHO DILIGENTLY CARE FOR THEIR PLANTS.

Ano di
same day leaf drop
a river bottom it
rotten, what
dat mean?

WHAT DAT MEAN?

A NUH SAME DAY LEAF DROP A RIVER BOTTOM IT ROTTEN:

THINGS CAN DETERIORATE GRADUALLY AND IMPERCEPTIBLY; THEREFORE, IT IS FOOLHARDY TO BE COMPLACENT AND TAKE PEOPLE OR THINGS FOR GRANTED.

ACTIVITY: FIND THE WORDS:

CAUTION
COMPLACENT
FOOLHARDY
GRADUAL
GRANTED
NEGLECT
PREVENT

```
G L J I E K Z S Y M
B R A H X S W C D F
P G A U R S A M R V
S S D N D U S L A N
K G A I T A L I H E
G S D I Y E R W L G
H Y O H J Q D G O L
T N E V E R P R O E
G O O I O L W A F C
C O M P L A C E N T
```

Yuh
waan good yuh
nose afi run, what
dat mean?

WHAT DAT MEAN?

YUH WANT GOOD YUH NOSE HAFFI RUN:
IN ORDER TO GAIN SUCCESS YOU HAVE TO WORK HARD.

ACTIVITY: ELLA'S ROAD TO THE CHAMPIONSHIP

INSTRUCTIONS:

IMAGINE A CHARACTER NAMED ELLA WHO DREAMS OF WINNING A REGIONAL SPELLING BEE. ELLA KNOWS THAT WINNING REQUIRES MORE THAN JUST NATURAL TALENT; IT DEMANDS HARD WORK AND PREPARATION.

WRITE A STORY ABOUT ELLA'S JOURNEY AS SHE PREPARES FOR THE SPELLING BEE. DESCRIBE THE CHALLENGES SHE FACES, THE STRATEGIES SHE EMPLOYS TO OVERCOME THEM, AND THE SACRIFICES SHE MAKES TO DEDICATE ENOUGH TIME TO STUDYING.

Alligator shouldn't call hag long mouth, what dat mean?

WHAT DAT MEAN?

ALLIGATOR SHOULDN'T CALL HOG LONG MOUT:

YOU SHOULDN'T BELITTLE OR CRITICIZE OTHERS WHEN YOU HAVE THE SAME FAULTS.

ACTIVITY: MIRROR MISTAKES

INSTRUCTIONS:

IMAGINE A CHARACTER NAMED SAM WHO IS QUICK TO POINT OUT WHEN HIS CLASSMATES MAKE MISTAKES IN MATH, HIS FAVORITE SUBJECT. HOWEVER, SAM STRUGGLES WITH WRITING, A SUBJECT HE FEELS INSECURE ABOUT.

WRITE A STORY ABOUT A DAY WHEN SAM CRITICIZES A CLASSMATE, LUCY, FOR A MISTAKE IN MATH, NOT REALIZING THAT HE WILL LATER NEED HER HELP IN A WRITING ASSIGNMENT.

Duppy know who fi frighten, what dat mean?

WHAT DAT MEAN?

DUPPY KNOW WHO FI FRIGHTEN:

BULLIES CAN DISTINGUISH BETWEEN THOSE THEY CAN INTIMIDATE AND THOSE WHO ARE BETTER LEFT ALONE.

Writing time

ACTIVITY: THE NEW KID AND THE PLAYGROUND CHALLENGE

INSTRUCTIONS:

IMAGINE A CHARACTER NAMED ALEX WHO IS NEW TO A SCHOOL AND NOTICES THAT THERE IS A BULLY NAMED JORDAN WHO SEEMS TO TARGET CERTAIN KIDS ON THE PLAYGROUND.

WRITE A STORY ABOUT ALEX'S OBSERVATIONS AND ACTIONS AS THEY LEARN MORE ABOUT JORDAN'S BEHAVIOR. EXPLORE HOW ALEX DECIDES TO HANDLE THE SITUATION WHEN JORDAN STARTS TO TEST THE BOUNDARIES WITH DIFFERENT STUDENTS, INCLUDING ALEX.

Same bird
weh carry news
come, a de same tek it
back. what
dat mean?

WHAT DAT MEAN?

SAME BIRD WEH CARRY NEWS COME, A DE SAME BIRD TEK EH BAK: THE SAME PERSON THAT BRINGS YOU GOSSIP WILL CARRY IT OUT.

Poem time

ACTIVITY: THE GOSSIP'S JOURNEY

INSTRUCTIONS:

THINK ABOUT HOW GOSSIP TRAVELS AND TRANSFORMS AS IT MOVES FROM PERSON TO PERSON. CONSIDER THE ROLE OF THE GOSSIP CARRIER, BOTH AS THE BRINGER AND THE SPREADER OF THESE STORIES.

WRITE A POEM THAT EXPLORES THE JOURNEY OF A PIECE OF GOSSIP. START WITH ITS ORIGIN AND FOLLOW ITS PATH AS IT IS WHISPERED FROM ONE EAR TO THE NEXT. REFLECT ON THE CHARACTERISTICS OF THE PERSON WHO SPREADS GOSSIP AND THE IMPACT IT HAS ON RELATIONSHIPS AND REPUTATIONS.

Shoes alone know if stocking hab hole, what dat mean?

WHAT DAT MEAN?

SHOES ALONE KNOW IF STOCKING HAB HOLE:
THOSE CLOSE TO YOU KNOW YOUR SECRETS.

ACTIVITY: WHISPERS IN THE WIND

INSTRUCTIONS:
.THINK ABOUT THE DYNAMICS OF CLOSE RELATIONSHIPS WHERE SECRETS ARE SHARED. REFLECT ON THE EMOTIONS TIED TO CONFIDING IN SOMEONE CLOSE AND THE TRUST THAT BUILDS FROM SUCH EXCHANGES.

WRITE A SONG THAT DELVES INTO THE INTIMACY OF SHARING SECRETS WITH SOMEONE CLOSE. EXPLORE THEMES OF TRUST, BETRAYAL, OR THE STRENGTH THAT COMES FROM SUCH VULNERABILITY. CONSIDER THE CONSEQUENCES OF THESE SECRETS BEING KEPT OR REVEALED.

Yuh tink
a suh parson get
him gown? What
dat mean?

WHAT DAT MEAN?

YUH TINK A SUH PARSON GET 'IM GOWN:

DO NOT BE ENVIOUS OF OTHER PEOPLE'S SUCCESS; YOU DONT KNOW WHAT THEY MAY HAVE GONE THROUGH TO ACHIEVE THEIR GOALS.

<u>ACTIVITY</u>: BEHIND THE CURTAIN OF SUCCESS

<u>INSTRUCTIONS</u>:

CONSIDER A CHARACTER, ANNA, WHO INITIALLY FEELS ENVIOUS OF HER CLASSMATE, MARK, BECAUSE HE ALWAYS SEEMS TO EXCEL EFFORTLESSLY IN SCHOOL, SPORTS, AND OTHER ACTIVITIES.

VERBALLY MAKE UP A STORY THAT DELVES INTO ANNA'S JOURNEY AS SHE LEARNS MORE ABOUT MARK'S LIFE BEYOND WHAT IS VISIBLE AT SCHOOL. EXPLORE THE STRUGGLES AND SACRIFICES MARK HAS MADE THAT ARE UNKNOWN TO OTHERS, WHICH CONTRIBUTE TO HIS ACHIEVEMENTS.

Bowl
go, packy
come, what dat
mean?

WHAT DAT MEAN?

BOWL GO, PACKY COME:

RETURN A FAVOR OR GOOD DEED BY DOING THE SAME.

<u>ACTIVITY:</u> THE CYCLE OF KINDNESS

<u>INSTRUCTIONS:</u>

IMAGINE A CHARACTER NAMED ELI WHO RECEIVES UNEXPECTED HELP FROM A NEIGHBOR, MRS. THOMPSON, DURING A DIFFICULT TIME. MRS. THOMPSON DOES SOMETHING TRULY KIND FOR ELI WITHOUT EXPECTING ANYTHING IN RETURN.

VERBALLY TELL A STORY ABOUT HOW ELI DECIDES TO REPAY MRS. THOMPSON'S KINDNESS. EXPLORE ELI'S THOUGHTS AND FEELINGS ABOUT THE GOOD DEED, HIS PLANNING PROCESS, AND HOW HE GOES ABOUT DOING A GOOD DEED IN RETURN.

Tu much ratta nebba dig gud hole, what dat mean?

WHAT DAT MEAN?

TOO MUCH RATA NEBA DIG A GOOD HOLE:

A GOOD JOB CAN BE RUINED IF THERE ARE TOO MANY INDIVIDUALS ATTEMPTING TO CARRY OUT THE SAME TASK OR IF EVERYONE ISNT PULLING THEIR WEIGHT.

Drawing time

ACTIVITY: TOO MANY COOKS

INSTRUCTIONS:

IMAGINE A SCENARIO WHERE A SCHOOL PROJECT IS ASSIGNED TO A GROUP OF STUDENTS. EACH STUDENT IS EAGER TO CONTRIBUTE, BUT SOON IT BECOMES CLEAR THAT HAVING TOO MANY LEADERS AND NOT ENOUGH FOLLOWERS IS CHAOTIC.

DRAW A SCENE FROM THE STORY DEPICTING A PIVOTAL MOMENT WHEN THE GROUP IS STRUGGLING WITH CHAOS OR WHEN THEY FINALLY FIND HARMONY IN THEIR ROLES.

No matta
how cockroach junk,
im noh waak pass fowl
yaad, what
dat mean?

WHAT DAT MEAN?

NO MATTA HOW COCKROACH JUNK, IM NOH WAAK PASS FOWL YAAD: WHEN YOU KNOW THE ENEMY YOU MUST AVOID THEM.

Mek
wan jackass
bray, what dat
mean?

WHAT DAT MEAN?

MEK WAN JACKASS BRAY:

DONT EVERYONE TRY TO TALK AT ONCE OR ADD TO THE CONFUSION.

<u>ACTIVITY:</u> THE CHAOS OF THE CLASS DISCUSSION

<u>INSTRUCTIONS:</u>

IMAGINE A CLASSROOM WHERE THE TEACHER, MR. BROWN, INTRODUCES A NEW AND EXCITING PROJECT. THE PROJECT SPARKS A LOT OF INTEREST AMONG THE STUDENTS, LEADING TO EVERYONE TALKING AT ONCE, EAGER TO SHARE THEIR IDEAS.

DRAW A SCENE FROM THE STORY SHOWING THE CHAOTIC MOMENT OF EVERYONE TALKING AT ONCE, OR THE CONTRAST WITH A LATER ORDERLY DISCUSSION.

Di older di moon di brighter it shine, what dat mean?

WHAT DAT MEAN?

DI OLDER DI MOON DI BRIGHTER IT SHINES:

OLDER PEOPLE GIVE BETTER ADVICE SINCE THEY'VE HAD MORE LIFE EXPERIENCE.

Drawing time

ACTIVITY: GRANDPA'S GARDEN WISDOM

INSTRUCTIONS:

IMAGINE A CHARACTER NAMED MIA WHO IS STRUGGLING WITH A DECISION ABOUT WHETHER TO JOIN A NEW CLUB AT SCHOOL OR STICK WITH HER OLD FRIENDS. UNSURE OF WHAT TO DO, SHE DECIDES TO SPEND A WEEKEND AT HER GRANDPARENTS' HOUSE.

DRAW A SCENE FROM THE STORY SHOWING MIA AND HER GRANDFATHER IN THE GARDEN, PERHAPS DURING A MOMENT OF PROFOUND ADVICE OR SHARED LAUGHTER.

Wen coco ripe, im mus buss, what dat mean?

WHAT DAT MEAN?

WEN COCO RIPE, IM MUS BUSS:
IT IS EASY TO IDENTIFY THE INTENTIONS OF AN INDIVIDUAL BY HIS/HER ACTIONS.

ACTIVITY: ACTIONS SPEAK LOUDER

INSTRUCTIONS:

IMAGINE A CHARACTER NAMED ALEX WHO IS RUNNING FOR STUDENT COUNCIL PRESIDENT. ALEX'S CAMPAIGN IS BASED ON PROMISES OF MORE AFTER-SCHOOL ACTIVITIES AND BETTER CAFETERIA FOOD. HOWEVER, ALEX'S ACTIONS AROUND SCHOOL SEEM TO TELL A DIFFERENT STORY.

WRITE A STORY ABOUT HOW ALEX'S CLASSMATES BEGIN TO UNDERSTAND HIS TRUE INTENTIONS THROUGH HIS ACTIONS RATHER THAN JUST HIS WORDS. DETAIL THE SPECIFIC ACTIONS THAT REVEAL HIS REAL MOTIVATIONS AND HOW OTHER STUDENTS REACT TO THESE DISCOVERIES.

Yu cyaan
sidung pahn cow
bak cuss cow kin.
What dat mean?

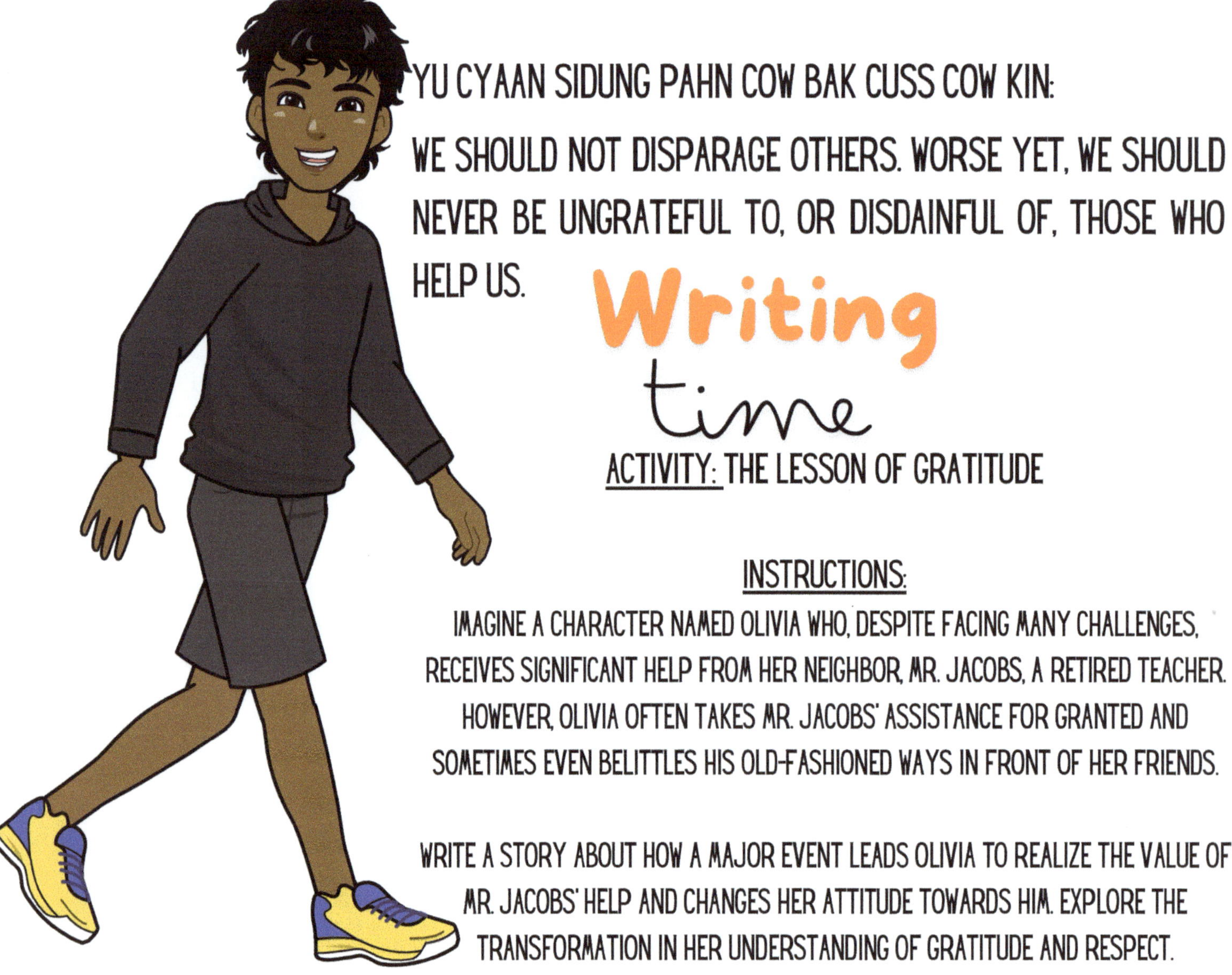

YU CYAAN SIDUNG PAHN COW BAK CUSS COW KIN:

WE SHOULD NOT DISPARAGE OTHERS. WORSE YET, WE SHOULD NEVER BE UNGRATEFUL TO, OR DISDAINFUL OF, THOSE WHO HELP US.

Writing time

ACTIVITY: THE LESSON OF GRATITUDE

INSTRUCTIONS:

IMAGINE A CHARACTER NAMED OLIVIA WHO, DESPITE FACING MANY CHALLENGES, RECEIVES SIGNIFICANT HELP FROM HER NEIGHBOR, MR. JACOBS, A RETIRED TEACHER. HOWEVER, OLIVIA OFTEN TAKES MR. JACOBS' ASSISTANCE FOR GRANTED AND SOMETIMES EVEN BELITTLES HIS OLD-FASHIONED WAYS IN FRONT OF HER FRIENDS.

WRITE A STORY ABOUT HOW A MAJOR EVENT LEADS OLIVIA TO REALIZE THE VALUE OF MR. JACOBS' HELP AND CHANGES HER ATTITUDE TOWARDS HIM. EXPLORE THE TRANSFORMATION IN HER UNDERSTANDING OF GRATITUDE AND RESPECT.

If yu
noh mash ants,
yu noh fine him guts.
What dat mean?

WHAT DAT MEAN?

IF YU NOH MASH ANTS, YU NOH FINE HIM GUTS:

IT IS ONLY WHEN YOU ARE CLOSELY INVOLVED WITH SOME PERSONS THAT YOU ARE ABLE TO REALLY KNOW THEM. IF ONE IS NOT PROVOKED, IT IS IMPOSSIBLE TO KNOW THE EXTENT OF HIS/HER FURY.

Song time

ACTIVITY: THE DEPTHS WITHIN

INSTRUCTIONS:

IMAGINE A CHARACTER NAMED THEO WHO HAS ALWAYS BEEN SEEN AS CALM AND COMPOSED BY HIS CLASSMATES. HOWEVER, HIS BEST FRIEND, MIA, SEES A DIFFERENT SIDE OF HIM WHEN A GROUP PROJECT PUTS UNEXPECTED STRESS ON HIM.

WRITE A SONG ABOUT THEO

Dead man tell no tales, what dat mean?

WHAT DAT MEAN?

DEAD MEN TELL NO TALES:
SOMEONE WHO IS DEAD CANNOT GIVE ANY INFORMATION TO ANYONE.

ACTIVITY: ECHOES OF THE PAST

INSTRUCTIONS:
IMAGINE A CHARACTER NAMED CLARA WHO DISCOVERS AN OLD DIARY BELONGING TO HER LATE GRANDFATHER, WHOM SHE NEVER MET. THROUGH THE DIARY, SHE BEGINS TO UNCOVER SECRETS ABOUT HER FAMILY'S PAST AND LEARNS ABOUT SIGNIFICANT HISTORICAL EVENTS THAT SHAPED HER GRANDFATHER'S LIFE AND, INDIRECTLY, HER OWN.

WRITE A POEM ABOUT CLARA

Pit inna de sky, it fall inna yuh y'eye, what dat mean?

WHAT DAT MEAN?

PIT INNA DE SKY, IT FALL INNA YUH Y'EYE:

WHAT YOU DO TO, OR WISH FOR OTHERS, COULD EVENTUALLY BE THE CAUSE OF YOUR OWN DOWNFALL.

ACTIVITY: THE BOOMERANG EFFECT

INSTRUCTIONS:

IMAGINE A CHARACTER NAMED ETHAN WHO IS KNOWN FOR HIS COMPETITIVE STREAK IN EVERYTHING FROM ACADEMICS TO SPORTS. WHILE ETHAN OFTEN WISHES FOR HIS PEERS TO FAIL SO HE CAN BE THE TOP OF HIS CLASS, A SIGNIFICANT EVENT MAKES HIM RECONSIDER HIS OUTLOOK

DRAW A SCENE FROM THE STORY SHOWING ETHAN EXPERIENCING A KEY MOMENT OF REALIZATION OR A SCENE WHERE HE MAKES AMENDS IN A SIGNIFICANT WAY.

New broom sweep clean, but owl broom noe dem cahna. What dat mean?

WHAT DAT MEAN?

NEW BROOM SWEEP CLEAN, BUT OWL BROOM NOE DEM CAHNA: YOUNG PEOPLE ARE INNOVATIVE AND THE OLD HAS VALUABLE EXPERIENCE.

Speaking time

ACTIVITY: BRIDGING GENERATIONS

INSTRUCTIONS:

IMAGINE A COMMUNITY PROJECT WHERE A LOCAL YOUTH GROUP AND A SENIORS' CLUB COLLABORATE TO REVITALIZE A NEGLECTED NEIGHBORHOOD PARK. THE YOUTH BRING THEIR ENERGY AND INNOVATIVE IDEAS, WHILE THE SENIORS CONTRIBUTE THEIR EXTENSIVE KNOWLEDGE OF THE COMMUNITY'S HISTORY AND GARDENING.

TELL A STORY ABOUT THE DEVELOPMENT OF THIS PROJECT, FOCUSING ON THE INTERACTIONS BETWEEN A YOUNG CHARACTER NAMED JAMIE AND AN ELDERLY CHARACTER NAMED MR. LEE. EXPLORE HOW THEIR INITIAL MISUNDERSTANDINGS AND DIFFERENCES GIVE WAY TO A FRUITFUL COLLABORATION.

Waant aal, lose aal, what dat mean?

WHAT DAT MEAN?

WAANT AAL, LOSE AAL:

TAKE JUST WHAT YOU CAN COMFORTABLY MANAGE, RATHER THAN ATTEMPT TO GRAB EVERYTHING FOR YOURSELF, LEST YOU DESTROY ALL IN THE PROCESS.

Speaking time

ACTIVITY: BAXTER'S BONE BONANZA

INSTRUCTIONS:

IMAGINE A DOG NAMED BAXTER WHO LOVES COLLECTING BONES MORE THAN ANYTHING. ONE DAY, BAXTER DISCOVERS A HIDDEN STASH OF BONES AT THE PARK. INSTEAD OF TAKING JUST A FEW, BAXTER DECIDES TO TAKE THEM ALL, DESPITE NOT NEEDING SO MANY.

TELL A STORY ABOUT BAXTER'S EXCESSIVE GATHERING OF BONES AND THE REPERCUSSIONS THAT FOLLOW. EXPLORE HOW BAXTER'S ACTIONS AFFECT NOT ONLY HIMSELF BUT ALSO OTHER DOGS IN THE NEIGHBORHOOD AND THE DYNAMICS AT THE LOCAL PARK.

WRITTEN & ILLUSTRATED BY:
DR. CORNELIA WALTERS-JONES
WEBSITE: DRCORNELIAWALTERSJONES.COM
EMAIL: LABRISH@JAMAICANGYAL.COM
CALL 876-836-0000

9 79833 0376230